Threads of Palestine Anthology:
Weaving Words of Witness

Threads of Palestine Anthology:
Weaving Words of Witness

Edited by Sara Bawany & Amal Kassir

House of Amal

House of Amal

Cover artwork, *The Ummah* by Safia Latif of © Safia Latif Paintings, used with permission. For more information, visit www.safialatif.com.

100% of the proceeds from the sale of this anthology will be donated to the Zakat Foundation of America, a non-profit organization dedicated to charitable work, helping communities in need, and promoting social justice around the world. For more information, please visit www.zakat.org.

For more information on House of Amal, please visit www.houseofamal.co and www.instagram.com/house.of.amal.

Publisher: House of Amal
ISBN: 979-8-9918907-0-0
Printed in The United States of America

For every martyr in Palestine, who lived and fought for their homeland. May our witnessing over the last year be the smallest justice in preserving your stories.

Table of Contents

Naomi Shihab Nye: Foreword 1

Introduction 5

Oliver Khan: Birds of Palestine 9

Shaziya Barkat: Broken Beams...11

Sana Nimer: Clutch Tightly Your Social Currency at the Cost of Moral Bankruptcy 12

Sundus Aladra: Fair Play 14

Layanne: Farewell, My Mother...16

Walid Kessal: For the Cause 18

Nehan Shujaat: Fossils of Olive Trees...20

Hajara Zaheed: Gazans Of Paradise..22

Jaweerya Mohammad: ghazal for gaza and genocide deniers.........................23

Zaheera Badat: Gaza Girl 25

Basheerah Bulbulia: Haunted 26

Amiira Afia: Death Certificate..27

Tajuddin Ashaheed: New Reservation...28

Kate Rafiq: Palestine is Palestinians 30

Hadee Krad: Red Black Green White 32

Yacoob Manjoo: Soldier's Fate...33

Nahida Izzat: The Beginning of the End 35

Naazia Husain Azhar: A Saturday in November.......................................36

Mariam M. Gadala: Young Hands 38

Wajiha Rizvi: An Atrocity in Three Acts 39

Sara Farhat: Dear World..42

Anam Fatima: Fireworks 44

Safiyah Zaidi: Frozen Over 46

Saniya Ahmed: I bear witness to heart failure..47

Salma Mohammad: ID Card 49

Noorul Hammad: From the Heart of Gaza 52

Noha Nasri: Rivers of Palestine 54

Warren Clementson: Split-Screen 57

Salma Alduais: The Gates of Every Home 59

Ray Lacina: Each Life Released, a Verse 60

Tehreem Khalid: Watermelon Season 61

Lana Kamel: What The Breeze Told Me...63

Nour Idris: Wondering: Sudan to Palestine 65

Hassan Hussein Ibn Ismail: Hope on the Horizon 67

Naqi Rizvi: Ya'aburnee 68

Anthology Producers and Editors 71

Anthology Artists 73

Contributors 75

Acknowledgments 83

About House of Amal 86

About Zakat Foundation of America 87

Foreword

By: Naomi Shihab Nye

Human

"I've come to think that if there is a single capacity or trait that distinguishes our species...it must be the imagination or the capacity to feel distress...to grieve...to rejoice."
— *W.S. Merwin, Poet*

Deepest gratitude to **House of Amal** for encouraging connection in the realm of honest voices. Thank you for offering a place for writers to express their collective and very particular grief, some better dreams and hopes, and to listen to one another. What a crucial gathering, in this despairing time on planet earth.

We're human. We're a species. We were born. What were we born to do?

Some of us were born into religious traditions and some were born into secular, ethical traditions, and some of us may feel like we were born into nothing but trouble and chaos. Basically, everyone probably believed "Thou shalt not kill" for a few idealistic moments here or there. If you were part of a religion, any religion at all, you heard it. *Do unto others. Treat them kindly. Otherwise life is even harder.*

And what do humans continue doing?

People don't say the word "greed" enough.
Slick chatter, seething vengeance, can cover up the simple word ***greed***.

What do you need? Where do you hurt?

Some people sanctify their own victimization—poor me, look what happened to my people, therefore I can do ANYTHING to you. Many of us heard ***Never forget*** while growing up. Did you? Did it apply only to one group of people?

1

"Humanity is beautiful when it comes together."
— *Thomas Jolly, Artistic Director of Olympics, 2024*

What happened on Oct. 7, 2023 was horrific, a tragedy beyond measure, conducted by desperate, oppressed (for 75 years) people—which does not in any way justify it. We grieve for all the dead and wounded on any "side" and wish none of it had ever happened to devastate so many lives. We are sorry beyond sorry. We also could have foreseen this oversized response, since there had been plenty of previous massacres in Gaza. When you have so many weapons, what else to do with them?

The official Gaza death toll currently exceeds 40,000, injury toll exceeds 92,000, thousands of traumatized children are reportedly wandering around unaccompanied, and the PTSD toll must tremble in the millions—more than 300 days of bombing and crushing and maiming, much of it paid for/donated by U.S. tax dollars and a majority of U.S. citizens who do not approve of such excessive vengeance at all. And no, it is not anti-Semitic to say this, especially since Palestinians are Semites too, so if one needs to lean on such terms, one could say every move made by Israel has been anti-Semitic since the beginning. I asked a historian why no one ever says this and he says the term was accepted long ago to apply only to one side of the conflict. But one could still ask, why?

When we were growing up, wars seemed like far away nightmares that humans should surely be willing to give up, now that we were farther from cave behaviors and knew each other better. Now that we have governments and diplomacy and languages, translators, educators, ways of instant communication, we could figure out better, more productive ways of engagement together. Dialogue, not monologue. Cease-fire talks that actually go *somewhere and make change*. The Dalai Lama says, "the impulse to try to solve problems by use of force is out of date and old-fashioned. Since we are all now so interdependent, the appropriate solution to engage is in dialogue – it's something to which we can all contribute." People in power don't even reference it often enough, as a center of possibility. My father always said all "peace talks" should happen around lots of food.

And poetry, literature, art, remains a major doorway to extended empathy. The grief over so many Gazan artists, writers, journalists, educators, people with precious skills and passions, being indiscriminately slaughtered, feels overwhelmingly painful. The children keep hoping and crying and trying to smile. It's what they were born for. Give them a balloon, an empty can and a stick. Give them a rag for a kitten's bed. Give them a song to sing, a circle to dance in.

Brave and adorable teenaged comics of Gaza, Omar and Mohammed, have their one million plus followers to console, but even they have confessed it's getting too exhausting. They wish none of this ever happened. They wish we never heard of them.

The poets who survive wherever we are keep writing and reading each other and wishing the people who make and supply weapons might think of something more imaginative to do. We're sad for every human who had no power in this matter. We're sad for every tree, every balcony and veranda, every crushed kitchen, and we feel like no one is listening to us. We are listening to one another, though—thank you again, House of Amal—and sometimes students around the world are listening to us, and hopefully the witness of writers occasionally penetrates the smoke and rubble with care. May the words in this book find many readers and offer consolation and connection.

A priest at my friend's funeral said, "There will be only one question on the final exam paper—how did you treat your neighbor?"

Naomi Shihab Nye, 2024

Introduction

Over the last year, much of the world has watched in horror the intentional decimation of Gaza in Occupied Palestine. Global media giants, not only excluding the voices of Palestinians, have also concealed anyone who may have compassion for the thousands upon thousands of individuals slaughtered by one of the most bloated militaries on planet Earth. There is a narrative that there are no people—except perhaps brown people and terrorists—who care about the Palestinian people. The theft of the voice of reason and human compassion is a deliberate media ploy that ensures humanity is only granted to one side of the conflict (the side that happens to have the most realtors, military contractors, and weapons), while the otherwise, essentially powerless side, is deemed barbaric, unworthy of life, and justifiable to be wiped off the planet.

Why would the mass media put so much effort into concealing a human narrative of the other side? Is it because words invoke a sense of truth? Is it because our hearts can be spoken into? Is it because, if the world knew not only of what was going on, but how the people of compassion felt about it, perhaps there would be a colossal uptick in those participating in boycotts and anti-war protests? At House of Amal, we believe so.

Feeling is so challenging right now, and what makes the poet so vital to the contemporary human experience is that they ensure that what is hard to feel is felt. The role of the poet is to use language in guiding us through this obscene darkness, beneath bombs and alongside grief and mass burials. Without knowing our pain, we are lost; foreign to our most human selves, destined for only vengeance and rage, not grief and compassion. The contributors of this book have done us the favor of helping us safely feel some of the heaviest emotions a bystander to multiple genocides could feel.

As a Muslim women-led writing organization, House of Amal has always been committed to both community and craft, with each component equally asserting itself in our day-to-day practice of teaching students, serving the needs of our community, and a commitment to accessibility. Right now, we are a shelter for the sacred voices that keep a corridor of the human heart alight.

Of this collective mourning have arrived poems, music, essays, stories, and more, born into the world in effort to preserve the memory of the hundreds of thousands martyred, to document in a world intent on ignoring, and to name who and what the occupiers are hellbent on erasing.

Activism and organizing can take many different forms, and as teachers and leaders committed to the multiplicity of this bravery, this anthology is one of our many commitments to doing so, although we don't stop here. We encourage everyone moved by the work in this book to commit to getting involved in the cause, to refrain from watering down and making palatable the meaning of liberation, but instead learn more about the history of Palestinian resistance and finding ways to support it.

We are proud to say that 100% of the proceeds for this anthology are going to charity. We have carefully selected Zakat Foundation to be the recipient of these funds to aid families in Gaza with medical assistance, food, hygiene kits, other essentials. We pray that this act of service is first and foremost accepted by Allah and that the words of our community offer a world of hope, justice, anger, and love towards this part of our ummah that is so greatly hurting.

Sara Bawany & Amal Kassir
House of Amal Team
Anthology Producers & Co-Editors

Oliver Khan
Birds of Palestine

> "Their souls are within green birds having lanterns suspended
> from the Throne, roaming freely in Paradise where they please,
> then taking shelter in those lanterns." – Hadith Qudsi 27

The martyrs of Palestine at first scatter
when God poses His question.
Their emerald wings

treading   through the air
making sunlight   swerve
in seven directions.

For the shortest   moment
their eyes are   darting,
tiny hearts   firing

like the cymbals of a riqq. They look up,
not knowing where they are, expecting to hear
turbines   sucking,

the whine   and whistle
of falling metal.
But instead, columns

of light   swim and   circle
the Throne in endless
murmurations   of praise.

God's question: *Do you wish for anything?*
They answer: *What could we*
wish for   *when we*
                    roam free
                    in Paradise?

God is quiet   amid the sound

of millions of wings   fluttering,
before asking   again.

They answer the same.
God asks   again. Some remember
Mama   drinking her morning coffee,

massaging her back   where the
children burrowed   into her
last night   when the sky was exploding.

Others remember   the soldiers tearing
down the neighbor's home. Some hear
Baba saying: *They arrested your cousin. They*
shot your uncle.   They

remember pulling   back the white
funeral shroud   for one last kiss. And

  one more.
            And one more.
                   Just one,
please.

      The birds beat their wings,
some sing   a warning, some are silent, some dive
into their lanterns, dark eyes blazing.

Then they plead one
after the other, *Oh Lord!*
Send us back.

Send us,
Oh Lord, back!
Send us back.

Shaziya Barkat
Broken Beams

If your heart quivers
with every cry from under the rubble
and your eyes weep
with every sunset drowned in white smoke.
if your gut churns
with every stomach that turns in hunger
and your hands raise
with every trembling child beneath the night's cloak –

embrace the pain you feel
for your heart is still alive.
A galaxy lies within your ribs.
The stars may burn, but thrive
by forcing light between the cracks
of your grieving, broken soul.
It's ok not to be whole.
It's ok.

This torch may seem too heavy
to carry in your chest sometimes.
Your heart aches as
buildings collapse –
smoke inflames the orbits of your eyes.
For every tear, a meteor's trail
beneath this vast, dim night.
For every murder, a comet's wail,
by black holes bereft of light.

Embrace the pain you feel,
for your heart is still alive.
Your feet are sore in tiny shoes,
lips parched with ragged sighs
pouring constellations into prayers
with palms raised like crescent moons.
With every ameen, a nova's flare
awaiting His justice to come soon.

Sana Nimer

Clutch Tightly Your Social Currency at the Cost of Moral Bankruptcy

Hold on to your purses
Your dollar's going for a ride
Stocks aren't dropping but bombs will!
Good news! You're hired! as Wall Street's mouthpiece
Job description: "remain reasonable"
Confident with a certain unwillingness to refuse
Comfortable that some content remain hidden from view
Content that *some prices* are worth paying, although
you'll never see the payout,
reserved for purses much bigger than yours
off-shore. Instead, keep your student loan debt
racking up double-digit percent interest
Keep stashing credit card points for that trip you'll take once
your days off as a cog are approved.

…Let's not talk about that now
Turn the radio up, you love that sound
That singer singing that song again about a love you'll never know
Cause your love…
this love…
it's silent.
It's subtle pining with a dollar sign in front of, not behind it
Call it heedlessness or greed?
In line for a tenth reusable cup
while death is thirst in line for water
Call it heedlessness or greed?
No occasion worth stopping for second thought
and no cost too obscene

Why not meet the moment,
this season of hedonism?
Why not decorate for its extremes
and hang Sidra's body on the wall.
Hang Sidra's half-maimed! mangled! body
missing her head! and little legs!
but retaining her jet black bowl cut bangs on the wall, but it's no longer
Halloween. No more than when
New Years passed with a blast after 95 days of blasts, an arrow
shooting towards a Valentine's Day that didn't last long for the husband

signing a love letter on the body bag of his wife.
His love...
was silent.

You couldn't hear it because the dollar sign was not in front of, but
behind it.
You couldn't hear it over the radio's drone
and over the lies you were sold.
What were the terms of your job contract? Did you
Read closely
You will never be able to fight
We will never be able to fight
until we internalize
that there is more to life
than this.
This, this
stuff
anchoring us to our places
better than any cage could.

Ensnaring us in the gains of life
Immobilized in opulence
Too addicted to caffeine to dream
of what might lie beyond espresso machines
Taste buds distracting us from the fact that

the belly of the beast
is rife with deliciousness.

But blood must always flow before one can eat meat.
Blood must always flow before the ravenous get their fill.
Blood always flows before anyone makes it in the belly of the beast
And wherever blood flows, there must be feast
Who is eating? Who is eating?
When another dawn rises on the dusty dry plates of refugees,
who of us is picking our teeth clean?
When it's in our hands to protect their blood from attack,
who of us is showing them our back?
Familiar transaction with a contactless tap?

In heedlessness and greed,
we pay taxes
but we do not pay tolls.

Sundus Aladra
Fair Play

Just be a good little Arab!
Palestinian? What's that?
Be a good little Arab; do what the nice
white man is telling you to do.
Just be a good little Arab
and we'll make sure to spare you.

      That's what they tell us day and night on the news
but what they won't tell you is that even when we
take their word for it
heed their warnings stamped on sheets of paper
dropped generously on us from the skies
      (while they simultaneously deprive us of everything
      we need to stay alive)
even when we play
by the intricate rules they lay
on the sadistic game board they paint
beneath our feet
we still lose
               every
                     time
     (and there is no finish line)

We anxiously wait for the world to awake,
to realize that the game is rigged
and that the nice white man lied —
but too many can't seem to see beyond the shine
of his fair hair and the twinkle of his blue eyes.

So we trip over
      our tracks
scrambling to find a third option —
hurtling through fiery rings of uncertainty,
trying to move fast enough to dodge the
      terror

aimed at us even in our sickness,
even in our sleep,
targeting our houses of God,
targeting our fleeing feet!
We play probability mind games to pick the safest place to hide,
theoretically,
pretending we don't know that in reality,
nobody escapes the crosshairs of the colonizer,

who won't sleep
until we cease —
        (to exist)

Just be a good little Arab!
they say,
After all, don't you want us to spare you?
Be a good little Arab...
Don't dream of independence
or safety.
What good does that do you?

Just be a good little Arab!
        (You're not a terrorist, now, are you?)
Don't go demanding justice
or freedom —
        (You don't look like us —
        You're not white like us, remember?)
— how could you?

Layanne
Farewell, My Mother

Where are you going?

To jannah, ya ummi.

But my children,
you are still young!
For what did I give you stones
of my body
that you may build homes
for your families
and terraces for your olive trees?

My children,
will you leave your homes empty?
What will become of the dreams
that dwelt with you;
the dreams that I fed
and helped grow?

My children,
who will sound the call to prayer,
my mountains are not able,
how will the earth
remember its Creator?

My children,
you are too young to go so soon;
I beg of you,
do not leave your villages empty,
do not leave this land,
your mother's embrace.

I am sorry, ya ummi,
we can stay with you no longer.
Our blood has been spilled,
ya ummi,
so now, to bear witness,
our souls must go.

Bullets may sever our skin
and tear us from your embrace,

but our existence,
none shall ever be able to erase.

Do not worry,
ya ummi,
our story is far from told.
We leave to you our bodies,
becoming seeds within your soil.

Spring always comes,
ya ummi,
and when it does,
those who live will remember,
and all the children of Palestine
will return to their mother.

Walid Kessal
For the Cause

sneaky rats   bite hard

spilt blood   stole land

injustice reigned   Resistance risen

    the occupation and the treason

tried   to stop the march of liberation

    breaking bones repression

forced pacifying

coming back every time   the Intifada kept rising

to dust off, to revive   the Resistance's sacred mission

to free the land   from the hands of occupation

    facing the law of the jungle that's ruling the world

"a rules-based order" ruling with double standards

the mighty nations have forced the acceptance of wrongs as good things

the justice is turned   half-blind, fully tied to be inconsistently applied

no sanctity of human rights   or peaceful resolutions

the law is only applied   against weak nations

let's stop this injustice   let's raise our voices

Screaming, Free Palestine   Free the oppressed peoples

    What's stolen by the weapons, can't be returned by demands.

this is Self-determination,   a struggle armed

against the tyrants

Freedom and Peace   always had a Heavy price

Paid In Blood   For The Cause

Nehan Shujaat
Fossils of Olive Trees

When something is written
and erased with the hard rubber of
time or oppression

even in its entirety —

know that nothing can be forgotten
if it leaves an imprint.

Similar to time, paper is unforgiving. There is
nothing you can erase from its surface
that won't come back to tell its story.

So who are we to think that one can eliminate
the history of people who still remember
what the sprouting of an olive seed
in the dirt smells like
or what the patterned fabric of resistance looks like
or how mothers went from worriers to warriors
or how fathers were ripped from their roots to
face an enemy who could not realize the irony
of eradication
or how children recognized too early
the cruelty this world holds?

No matter how many times
you erase someone's pain
it will return
in the form of art —
it will bleed like the fragrance of jasmines
in the hottest summers
and rise like wings from fire in bitter winters.

You see —
when you write with a pencil, the pressure

of words never leaves paper
no matter
how much you force the graphite away.
There is a dent left forever,
with grooves that still
remind you of its presence.

You will always be left
with the fossilized trace
that something was always there.
The irreversible miracle of memory cannot be
stolen from its owner.

We still remember who they are and where they came from,
no matter how many times one tries to disregard
truth and identity.

We know that they are made to last, to withstand
the dishonesty of oppressors.
Surely there is
something that will be left of them even when
there is nothing left of them.

We will remember because the stones will speak about how
they too fought amongst the believers,
and the sky will testify that it witnessed
bombs pierce its paper-thin skin.

Nothing is hidden from our Maker,
and nothing can be pulled from its root without a
certainty it won't grow again.

We should ask now, how many trees
have to be brutally
killed for these words to
scream at us on their paper?

Hajara Zaheed
Gazans Of Paradise

You let out a sigh, once again you've survived.
Through the rubble, familiar voices draw nearer.
You close your eyes, draw a long breath,
wishing things were how you remember;

Sailors and their seas, farmers preparing the soil,
the children singing alongside the laughter of sunbirds.
Neighbors and their stories of your father pressing olive oil,
love and compassion was the language your son learnt —

You open your eyes and take in what you see.
You've been rescued to rejoin a world of catastrophe
left with animal feed, dead bodies, tent scraps,
and a dying hope of what could be if your homeland is returned back

Blood streaked walls border every street.
The aftermath of every attack leaves a terrible taste.
But war-torn towns have dreams to safekeep,
so despite the displacement, you stand full of praise.

You roam what is left of the gardens of Palestine.
Olive groves and lemon trees grow into mass graves.
You know your home is among the gardens of Paradise.
With His remembrance you remain a grateful slave.

Teaching restraint while treating the pain,
With utmost compassion you console —
"Hold on a little longer, for just a little more remains"
Hold on until it is called upon believing souls;

> *"Welcome and rejoice, Oh Gazans of Paradise!*
> *Behold your reward for all you endured.*
> *Welcome and rejoin the Martyrs of Palestine!*
> *Eternity is yours, by the grace of your Lord."*

Jaweerya Mohammad
ghazal for gaza and genocide deniers

the arabic word used to refer to those who have died in sacrifice is
shaheed;
more than a martyr, its root also means to bear testimony or to witness.

my phone, weighted messenger in my palm, lights up and screams a
splinter
of a soundbite. from thousands of miles away my entire living room bears
witness.

a boy rubs the belly of a white wild-eyed cat, her brittle hair
like prickly spines, her meowing muted from the missiles witnessed.

the women knead and press palms into dough, carefully baking costly
bread,
the sagging bag of flour in the corner, wet with blood, is witness.

bride and groom clasp hands in a schoolhouse turned shelter, grasping
for a slice of joy. in this union of resistance, the dancing children are
witness.

a man coated in ash, scrapes away rubble with fingernails only to find
the scarf of his mother, green and white, still scented like the shaheed.

four infants, wrapped in sheets at a hospital decompose, the hissing
respirators
now silent, a journalist was witness; before him the stray dogs were
witnesses.

the ground, against her will, soaks up blood and swallows small bones only
to be dug up and spit out again. she will retaliate, the passing clouds are
her witness.

the sheep, the stones, the strawberry fields, the olive trees, the air soiled
with smoke, all weep witnessing the stories shuddering at the lips of the
shaheed.

do the dying record and plead for dignity when they are inheritors of
whiteness,
thin pink flesh is so easily believed, so easily beholden to, without any
question of witness?

justice always finds her vessel, bursts out like water from a broken dam
gushing giant waves,
i wish for her frothing wrath to engulf you, watch your mouth split aghast
in witness.

Zaheera Badat
Gaza Girl

We see you —
in the single

thread
of
transmission

that links
our daily
to the noose around your voice.

In the two hundred milliliter ration meant to
sustain your living.
In the empty orbits that cradle
broken bodies
blasted brains
burnt babies.
In the rubble graveyards and hospital heaps —

we see you.

Close your eyes, Gaza girl.
Relinquished
of everything
but your fight.

Close your eyes, thirsty girl.
Drink deep
from the pools of paradise.

Basheerah Bulbulia

Haunted

If stones could speak
they'd roar in outrage
at the gardens built upon graves.

Come,
lay a blanket under a tree.
Tell your children about this cemetery.
That the crunch beneath their feet
is the crushing of bones
and the whispers of the wind
mourn a motherland.

Tell your children,
the grass they play on
grew from the tears of a mother,
ripped from the grave of her son.

Tell your children to be gentle;
this garden's stones mark tombs —
their footsteps might disturb the dead.

And you wonder why you are haunted...

Amiira Afia
Death Certificate

her death certificate is handed to her father
before the certificate of her birth can even be
printed. the world demands proof of their
suffering so he lifts her body as evidence of
her existence. how much cloth does one need
for the shroud of a newborn baby? if she is so
tiny, why does lowering her in the grave feel
so heavy? these are everyday matters in the
land of sea breeze and olive trees. if you know
what is in store for you, you'd be begging for
forgiveness at their feet. we all know this
didn't start on the seventh of October. how
can you believe these lies over and over? their
soil may be soaked in blood, and broken glass
in place of mud. but remember, you cannot
kill a people who know true life begins at the
very last breath. because for the believer, real
freedom and success emerges from death.

Tajuddin Ashaheed

New Reservation

Welcome to the New Reservation,
Where Palestinian is synonym
For "Native American."

Where Gaza is but a Steri-Strip,
Slapped on a bullet wound.

Where mortar shells smack-smack into the bricks,
And the people barely fit.

Where the kettle is bound
to boil over real soon.

Where freedom dies like buffalo in silence,
While future lives are victim to the addiction of violence.

Just how do you live in a city where you must sell
The broken parts of your neighborhood,
That have been repeatedly shelled,

Bombed out and torn down,
Where the word "building" is always a verb,

And never a noun?

Where schools and masjids are smoldering has-beens,
Where the cityscape is scorched out stubble,
And people buy food by recycling the rubble?

Over here, the natives are given "reparations" of casinos and payday loans,
In 'Ghazzah they only have
Slingshots and their mothers' tears.

Stuck like Old Testament Hebrews
In between Egypt and the Sea,
Bricks mortared by the concrete of despair and misery.

Neither neighbors nor the water provides any relief,
Sabra and Shatila are today's Wounded Knee and Sand Creek.

If we consult the past to see the future unfold,

We all know Pandora's box holds very little hope.

Life in the Strip stays a sad ballad
Of tear gas canisters and full metal jackets,
Suicide runs, retaliation, and
Adolescent martyrdom.

Where Sons are taught to die young
Because War is the only thing left to live for.

They want jobs but not an occupation.
They're not looking for casinos or bucktooth sports logos
To trade for their assimilation.

So, they try to sleep the sleep of giants,
To dream the dreams of Philistines.

Every fingertip is a wick, lighting
Hookah pipes and dynamite.

The people pray for rain daily
To wash away the pain but
What comes from the Rivers of Sorrow is the only moisture they get.

The same bitter water drank by Geronimo that made him immortal.

Do they remember the lessons that the Old Books taught?
Do they remember the ancient Gaza that Samson walked?

Do they see his hands pushing and pushing on the pillars,
Because the reservation is rapidly running out of room?

They are pushing and praying,
Praying and pushing,
While the people are dancing in the pavilion, oblivious and blind.

They don't see the pushing.
They don't hear the prayers.

No! they're still dancing in the pavilion,
Oblivious and blind.
They don't see the hair on Samson's head that's starting to grow back.

So, they don't hear the roof above them that's starting to crack.

Kate Rafiq
Palestine is Palestinians

I don't have the words to describe my raging heart,
I don't think the right words exist in any language,
And every time I start to write, my thoughts are blown to pieces,
By the news of more bombs dropped on my Palestinian siblings,
And their babies of all ages, from the unborn to the ancient.
Now twelve thousand dead at least and more trapped under concrete.
The dust fills the gaps and surely they can't see.
The dust fills their lungs and for sure they cannot breathe.
And even after decades being detained, starved, squeezed,
Occupied and forced from a land their hearts won't leave.

Palestine is Palestinians —

from the river to the sea.

I don't have the words to define this seething grief,
But the English that I know is the keeper of the key.
It's the master of the mayhem, artist of anarchy,
With its map and sharpened pencil, it draws catastrophe.

And all the so-called leaders sit in shameful wretched silence,
Rejecting calls for ceasefire, with their beastly suited violence.
As fathers dig through rubble to raise their buried babes,
Their perfect arms and legs, inscribed with their names.
"They brought it on themselves!" We're told that they're to blame.
It seems that killing unarmed kids is just part of the game.
The hands of colonizers pat each other on the back
As they bomb them, crush them, break them down,
Then bomb them as they push them south,
Bomb them in the hospitals,
Bomb them in the schools and camps,
Bomb them, shoot them, bomb them more.
Refusing to ceasefire, but considering 'a pause'.

I don't have the words; there's no way to describe
The evil that suggests 'a pause' in genocide.

Perhaps they think it's time for some warm East India tea,
While they draw more lines on maps to destroy humanity.
But no matter what they do — and what they fail to see —

Palestine is Palestinians —

from the river to the sea.

Hadee Krad
Red Black Green White

Red for the blood of thousands of kids.
Black for the souls of those who committed this.
Green for the last standing olive trees.
White for the gates in heaven, overflowing.

Yacoob Manjoo
Soldier's Fate

Bang! Bang! Bang!

Another (tiny) terrorist dead —
toddlers a 'grave threat'
to cowards in combat gear
who wreak wanton destruction
on all they encounter
in this blessed land,
already besieged for decades,
yet now facing extinction —
natives not welcome,
as the children of darkness
seek annihilation,
lusting after precious beachfront property
which beckons
when this land is "cleaned up".

Bombs snatch childhood in an instant,
Gaza's schools no longer a place of learning.
No longer a place at all —
destroyed
by the targeted missiles
of cold-hearted killers
looking for phantom tunnels.

Gaza's hospitals are no longer havens for healing.
Instead, monuments of massacres,
as real-life monsters stalk the halls
looking for any moving creature to mow down.
Murderous munitions unlimited
as foreign tax dollars
freely fund this façade of self-defense.
"No red lines"
in this war of extermination.

To you, fearless soldier, we say:
kill,
kill,
and kill some more.
Stay intoxicated,
deluded by the deception of your war machine.

Think not
of the grave threat
that awaits you tomorrow —
fitting payment for your atrocities:
a hole of horrors, pain and sorrow.

For every soul shall taste death.
And if the sounds of slaughter
don't haunt you in this world,
be sure
that your memories of murder
will torment you in the next.

Because when it all fades to black,
when the veils of deception fall down,
you'll stare in horror,
eyes fixed
at the fate you've earned.

No leaders to take the fall
in your stead.
No lies to hide behind,
only fear and dread.

You'll be
just a single soul
all alone
about to face terrors far worse
than those you so glibly dished out
when you had the power
to choose differently.

But that's just the appetizer:
a small taste of the torment awaiting
in your abode of eternal (un)rest.

So, know
that whether or not you care,
your soul will be ensnared.

Divine Justice awaits.
Rush forward,
meet your fate.

Nahida Izzat
The Beginning of the End

This is not the last battle.
This is not the final blow.
And yet again
we made the u-turn.
This is the road with no return —
a pivotal battle on the path of liberation.

Just read the writing on the wall.

Be prepared for the ugly.
More grief and pain.
But at the end
the light is glowing
showing the way.

Come face your fears.
Come break your chains.
From wombs of agony
life is born.

The birth of a baby
takes incredible energy.
Patience, courage and willingness to sacrifice
one's comfort, sleep, normality
and even one's own life.
A mother goes through unimaginable pain
and it gets more acute
towards the end.
But then,
before we know it
life is born.
The first breath is taken.
A baby screams
bringing joy and relief.
Mama and Baba cry.
Such is Freedom.

Naazia Husain Azhar
A Saturday in November

Today I have:
        One Boy Scouts meeting
Two soccer games
        Three birthday parties

It is busy in the fall
        Why am I here,
When my siblings are in Gaza

        I cry in my car
And I wonder
        Is everyone else crying
In their cars too
        As we drive from one luxury
To the next?

        If my tears could travel
I would take them to Palestine now
        And wash the dust and blood
From a child's face
        A child who survived
While his entire family has not
        I would wash away every trauma

As the car tears intensify,
        Loud, ugly, desperate, ashamed
Why do we cry for Karbala,
        I start to understand

        I park at the soccer field,
We sing happy birthday,
        The leaves are changing color,
Fall was always
        My favorite season

How can I
        Sip pumpkin spice privilege
While my siblings are
        Crushed under rubble

Tonight:
        I will not sleep well
I will bear witness
        I will tell my children.

Mariam M. Gadala
Young Hands

Innocent eyes
reflect betrayal.
Prison walls
envious of birds
allowed to fly.

Young hands
planting olive trees,
& seeds of dreams;
the same young hands
reaching out
to the stench of silence
from beneath rubble,
only to grasp
air.

Wajiha Rizvi

An Atrocity in Three Acts

SOUNDSTAGE - GAZA - NIGHT
                    Act I

                    DIRECTOR
          Places, everyone! Can we get some more
          blood for this man's shrapnel wound?

The sound mixer turns up the atmospheric buzzing
of the drone overhead.

          Where are the white phosphorus burns?
          Make sure there's exposed bone in the
          shot. Can the little girl take her
          place — the one who's wise beyond her
          years because she's had to grow up too
          fast?

When the infant exits stage right — lips purple
and blue, body swollen and yet also wrung dry
like the carcass of a lemon — he will open his
eyes and give his mother a smile. She will pull
the once limp body close, whispering, *you did so
well for one so young, my darling.*

His coos usher the warmth back into his cheeks.
When he learns to speak, she will teach him to
say Hasbunallah wa ni'mal-Wakil. The audience
will wonder at the child's faith and their
hearts will break as their outrage intensifies.

Twentysomething reporters fresh out of college
are the cinematographers.

                    The director shouts
          More anguish! Your leg was just blown
          off! I didn't believe your screams.

SUBURBAN HOME - AMERICA - MORNING
Act II

The bloodshed we've seen on our screens is a
limited series of unknown duration. Each episode
uploaded as we sleep, leaving the audience
wondering whether the carnage will be renewed
for another season.

   The hospital siege episode broke me,
I heard someone tell a friend.

   I'm pretty sure all the best
   characters will die in the end. Bisan is my
   favorite. I can't wait to see what she does
   next.

When it gets too intense I put my phone away,
screen facing down. Every day is a different war
crime. A targeted UNRWA school. Demolished
multi-story flats. It takes as much skill to
direct the subtlety of the devastation as it
does to act it out.

But a self-imposed genocide in three acts makes
more sense than setting my convenience up in
flames. So if you tell me our pain doesn't
exist, I'll believe you. I'll question the
carnage in front of me without your prompting
and I'll say they had it coming. I'll have a
counterclaim for every war crime allegation. I
guarantee it will be more convincing than
anything you could feed me.

The five imperialist food groups have lined my
stomach since childhood: doubt, denial, self-
loathing, division, shame.

Perhaps Act III's anticipated conclusion won't
occur until after I'm gone.

Maybe the Palestinians' valor will be the topic
of a series finale for another generation.

Maybe that generation will charge through the
screens and demand a supporting role.

May they atone for the sins of the spectators
gone before.

Act III

...

Sara Farhat
Dear World

Dear World,

am I not human?
my flesh and identity

unwanted?
haggard, hated; a hazard

sign drapes me
sharp stares suffocating me.

World, don't my roots originate from you?
yet you uproot me

then tell me
I'm causing the chaos?

didn't you cast a dark lens
on me,

stranding me?
World, wasn't it you?

who labels and dismisses
which lives matter

pointing fingers at me
saying I am to blame?

while my home
burns in flames

when it comes to me
you become blind.

am I not one of yours?
a part of your backbone

crushing and crumbling
dislocating me at sea.

didn't you plant me?
tell me to grow

and then cut my flowers.
didn't you make me bare and barren?

displace and sever me
as my unaccepted blood escapes

World, am I not your captive?
confining me with your judgement

depriving me of a name
and identity

weren't you who birthed us to give us homes?

inviting me to live.
World, am I not your resident?

who do I call home then,
if that's not you?

Anam Fatima
Fireworks

Watching fireworks from my balcony,
Was always a moment of glee.
But today every flickering spark,
Is a reminder of an unabated tragedy.

Fireworks lit up the heavens,
Marking an occasion of festivity.
But the blazing sky of Palestine,
Is reminiscent of horrific realities.

Fireworks that attract awe and admiration,
Now add to the chaos and bewilderment.
Reducing to rubble every familiar abode,
From safety and security, forced estrangement.

Heart-wrenching visuals fail to stir the dead conscience,
Power-occupiers too unsound and bent on destruction.
Swapping positions, tasting their own medicine,
Can only compel them to stop the endless violence.

These pretty fireworks will light up and go silent,
But what about the bombings that go on unabated.
What about the helpless screams that make the earth shudder,
Surgeries performed, without anesthesia, limbs amputated.

Massacres upon massacres endlessly committed,
Days pale and cruel, nights lit up in fiery horror,
Starvation and deprivation, arduous tests of time,
Striving to survive despite everything broken and blurred.

Woe to the so-called leaders, who could have saved lives,
Hoodwinking the world by the firecrackers of distraction,
Changing the headlines to their own selfish motives,
Every atom of the earth witnessed their disdain & inaction.

Every family torn apart, will be reunited in Jannah,
Every wound and suffering will be compensated.
Gates of Heaven will open with beautiful sparks,
They will be welcomed with 'Peace' and ranks elevated.

Fireworks have ceased now, in this part of the world,
Sky is dark and smokey; kids are tired and happy.
Lips murmur with prayers, heart is still heavy,
Indeed we, the Muslim ummah, are one body.

Safiyah Zaidi
Frozen Over

In the days after, a coldness seeps in.
The retreat is swift, the battle lines absolute.
They on one end,   I on
The other.

Recrimination and redress,
apology and answer –
I chant my mythology and they chant theirs.
They become incantations, each desperately trying to undo the other.

These are sounds
emptied of meaning / plundered of history / stripped of memory.

It is said that we warm our hands by the same fire,
But there is a man burning through my streets.
I walk by his pyre, jeers echoing in my ears.

Disbelief at this callousness,
It subsides into limp resignation,
Then crests into a cold rage.
There can be – *should be* – no warmth in this world

while Gaza dies.

Saniya Ahmed
I bear witness to heart failure

She sits at her desk   day eclipsing   into night   as I am kept

trapped and quiet   between ribs   the boy whispers the

shahada to his baby brother   coaxing the words to his tongue   so he is

comfortably welcomed   Home   the newly orphaned babies

cry   ringing grief into the air like   missiles piercing clouds

          doctors discover their own families   deceased   as

bodies are brought to emergency floors   parents carry

martyrs within the palm of their hands   I cry out

          wounded from the shrapnel   aching as limbs are pulled out

from under the rubble carrying parts of my own youth   in plastic

bags   she tries to bury me   in the spine of her books   crushed

between pathogens   and complement cascades   as if

the infectious injustice   could be fixed by simple clotting   as if

pharmacological agents   need memorizing   when phosphorous

bombs eradicate entire classes of schoolkids   she turns off

her socials   as internet cuts out in Gaza   to isolate without escape

          she wants to focus   on building illness scripts as buildings fall

aflame   on her sisters and brothers   I weigh heavy on her lungs

          and the cavity fills with the blood of our people   she winces

at every breath   reminded that humanitarian hospital rounds

          don't have ceasefire   so neither can her slow loss of humanity   she drowns in survivor's guilt   suffocated

by systems she operates in   that remove her   from

herself   and from her people   it is easier to divide

and conquer   to sequester into confines of professionalism

          that push her into complacency   she fails exams   and

her people   her mind and heart stretched   across oceans her

scarf soaking   the wounds of the Ummah   her

soul sutured   to the hands of humanitarian healthcare   her

revolution is in the turmoil   of keeping her head down

to survive and study   when all I want is   to serve

          my people on the frontlines   to stand   against

oppression everywhere   to mourn   the realities of those

enduring   and make endless dua'a   for liberation and lives

martyred   someone said that successful completion   of steps to

become a doctor   is a pledge   to help my communities   in the

future but   wombs become tombs   and I worry what

community   will be left   by the time we gain enough power   and

what is our worth   if not for our people   we joined medicine

to heal   not to be held   from truth   and I titrate her soul into

reality   staining her white coat   with fatigue and pain and

remembrance   and shackle her stethoscope to   myself

so while the world may suffer from heart failure   we   will remain

alive.

Salma Mohammad
ID Card
after Mahmoud Darwish

"Write down!
That I am Palestinian."
My ID Number is 50,001.
My mother was harvested in Nablus
next to trees of teen —
the roots of the plants here match the scars on her body.
They have both bled for this land.
Do you know your roots?
Or do you just pillage ours?

Do the hearts you hurt haunt you?
You pile children on top of dead mothers
and for the rest of their lives
they try to carve love out of the rubble made of their homes.
You've made firework displays
of Friday prayers
and watch as communities plant graves under olive trees.
You censor the world of Palestine's pain
and force us to heal in lands we are foreign to.
Do you even remember my mother?
She holds the weight of this country.

You ask of my eyes.
They lay witness to your violence and will speak on your trial with God
The olive trees lay witness to you.
The doves lay witness to you.
The rubble lays witness to you.
And on your trial with God, they too will defend us.
You have tried to make the world blind to us,
but we scream, we sing, we dance.
We are seen beyond the eyes and
heard beyond the ears.
Our souls will never submit to your oppression.
You are foreign to this land, but this land will never forget
the people who fought for it
take my body,
take my ID card,
take my home, and my family,
but you can never take my identity.

You ask who I am—
ask the bricks instead.
I am my mother's child,
the spine
that carries the testament of our resistance
the legacy of our land that raises
Nablus farmers
Unbreakable leaders
Revolutionary poets.
Quiffyah-wearing, olive-oil-sweating, thick-browed, fig-eating
Palestinians.
We are ID-ed by—
the way our voices rattle the mountains
the way our tears plant gardens instead of graveyards
the way our hope sustains generations.

You ask of my family.
when you rob our children of their limbs.
All this time you have had to dissect us, and yet you have not learned
that Palestinians don't die.
We are reborn as an echo
that tells our families we will be home.
That tells our children to persist in their resistance,
that tells the world our keys cannot be taken,
for the keys to Palestine are documented in our kin.
The tongues that passed down our history,
the hands that embroidered our spirit into our clothing,
the eyes that refuse to ignore the pain they have seen,
and the arms that defend our homeland.

"Write down!
That I am Palestinian."
I do not need an ID card because you know who I am.
I am a threat.
My identity is not something you can take and give as you please,
my identity will never
leave my tongue
leave my family's eyes
leave my mother's limbs
leave Palestine's soil.
We are heard in the the echoes of Revolution's trachea.
And upon my return to Palestine
I will wear my mother's scars as my armor

and I will walk a path of rebuilt bridges
Revived by the stories of our families
as we return home
where the key will always fit.

Noorul Hammad
From the Heart of Gaza

A mother's gaze on her newborn's corpse,
she holds him close, a painful pause.
Bidding farewell when she dreamt of embrace,
It's a devastating loss, in this sorrowful space.

A brother, right beside his sibling in despair,
He shares the burden of a world unfair.
In whispers,he encourages them to hold on,
Though life is fleeting, hope is never gone.

A confused child asks why her parents won't respond,
Frightened with the chaos from all around.
Amidst the screams and cries, her small voice pleas
Seeking answers from a world too blind to see.

Bodies crushed beneath the rubble's weight,
Desperation fuels a father's relentless state.
With a heavy heart, he hammers all through the night,
To rescue his loved ones in the fading light.

The healthcare frontier stand so strong,
Saving lives unconditionally, all day long.
As they serve their duty, there is no time to mourn,
Their loved ones are gone, from this world so forlorn.

Brave Journalists unveil the truth at life's stake,
They capture all the suffering, for justice's sake.
Targeted by the Oppressor, their voice almost muffled,
Still, they persist, despite every struggle.

In the face of such anguish, our hearts can't remain still.
We must rise together, with unbreakable will.
For every mother's tears, for every child's plea,
For every brother's courage, let our spirits be free.

For every father who strives through the darkest of nights,
We must lend our strength, be his guiding lights.
For every healthcare warrior, for every journalist so brave,
Their sacrifices honored, their stories we'll share.

Stand against the tyranny, the cruelty, the pain,
For the world must not ignore, nor witness in vain.
Together, we can end this horror, this plight,
For the world must act now, and stand up for what's right.

Noha Nasri
Rivers of Palestine

Ya Falasteen,

It was 2000 when I wrote my first poem for you,
about children tripping over bloody limbs
on their way to school.

It's 2023 and over 20,000 have been killed.
There are no more schools.

Rescue heroes tripping over the bodies of bloody children.
There are no more children;
only souls witnessing hell on earth.

Your land drowns in the stench of genocide,
and politicians hide behind blind eyes,
denying a cease fire.

My heart bleeds
but it's your blood on the streets.

You are the rivers
that nourish the Motherland.

Your blood drained
into the veins of Palestine.

There are no kisses good night,
only bombs forcing goodbyes.

Children identified
by the names written on their arms.
If they are still attached.

I scream in bloodcurdling dreams
about your reality.

Ya Falasteen,

You are angels in the form of humans;
too pure for this earth.

Your men murdered while consoling orphaned children
burned by white phosphorus.

Skin marred by
the dried blood of a thousand victims.

Cries for cease fire
fall on deaf ears.

But we hear you.

Your trials are our tribulations.
How can I stand before God,
 if I did not at least speak for your freedom?

I pray for your children to hold books
instead of the bodies of their mothers;

in search of knowledge
instead of mutilated siblings under rubble.

if you kill one person
it's as if you've killed all of humanity.

They've murdered over 10,000 of your people in 30 days,
this math I can't comprehend,

so tell me,
are we dead or alive?

Oh Children of Adam,
if you have a voice, call for ceasefire.

Ya Falasteen,
your rivers will flow free.

Warren Clementson
Split-Screen

My family and I ~~have no choice but to~~

sit back ~~stay where we are~~

and watch a ~~genocidal~~

drama. My children ~~are too exhausted to~~

curl up next to me, appreciating the moment ~~when their souls will finally~~

~~relax.~~

The conclusion approaches, ~~emptied~~

eyes glued to the screen. It's ~~not~~

how we thought it would be. My wife begins to ~~scream as the rockets~~

laugh; ~~praising God one last time,~~

my son closes his eyes, ~~ready to leave this life.~~

My daughter ~~goes limp,~~

lays still on the sofa ~~as I hear the army of the undead.~~

Gaza

~~(dis)~~

appears in my mind. I

~~try to~~

block it out —

Salma Alduais
The Gates of Every Home

even when the world
ignores your pleas

even when its people
fail you time and time again

know these scars
are a testament
to your faith —
etched into the heart
of every child
longing
for their homeland

surpassing generations

where olive trees
continue to adorn
the gates
of every home
with power

creating beauty

out of remnants
that mark strength
like no other

Ray Lacina
Each Life Released, a Verse

in a poem of a thousand stanzas
in a book of a thousand pages.
The Children of the Olive Groves
taken down from the high shelf
held in your lap
by the window
where you sat with mother
once, on a night
when the world was gray with rain
when the night's lament
was only the rattle of rain.

rest your cheek
against this page
where it's rested before
breathe deep the scent
of mother's hands
of vellichor.

and after the ordinance
falls
and the night turns to red flame
anguish
the night's lament cries out.

each page curls black
each verse flame-bit
flensing smoke fills
your throat
and coiled above the burning block
each floating ember cools
to ash
each gasp
burns.
burns

the missile's fall
the burnt page
the reek
the smokey night's lament
this devil's vellichor.

Tehreem Khalid
Watermelon Season

It's the season of the watermelon
all the curtains have fallen
all devils are set free
death rains down incessantly

It's the season of the watermelon
reality is being unveiled
lurking shadows are revealed
morally forthright are rioting

It's the season of the watermelon
the brutalizing of bodies
the killing of spirits
the burial of those still living

It's the season of the watermelon
their vines are spread far and deep
you think your hatred could bury them
but their seeds will flower again in spring

It's the season of the watermelon
red, black, white, and green
the burning of the olive trees
the souls lost to a genociding

It's the season of the watermelon
the land that grew strawberries
the sunset adorned her beaches
the courage that never seems to dim

It's the season of the watermelon
it's the voices screaming in the streets
"From the river to the sea,
Palestine will be free"

It's the season of the watermelon
it's when the skies were set on fire
it's when every picture revealed the story
yet the world remained unmoving

It's the season of the watermelon
it's when all hearts became agitated
when there was no one left to turn to
"Hasbunallahu wa ni'mal wakeel."

It's the season of the watermelon
it's Motaz, it's Bisan, it's Reem
it's every heart that once was beating
the ones entrapped set the world free

Lana Kamel
What The Breeze Told Me

There is a breeze

which carries the memories of this vacant land
from one yearning soul to the next
from generations kneaded into its grain
to generations that come,
forming a clot of its hope.

It whispers weakly into my ear…

I grew up in this land.
I've memorized every wrinkle in her soul.

I can tell you the details you do not recall.
I can tell you about her olive trees,
who cradled me in loneliness and nourished me back to life;
who speak a tongue with my mother
as though their beings could not help but intertwine.

I know her fruits are tied to this land,
like we were her children —
her best friend.

You and me, the breeze.

I can tell you about the colors that filled these streets.
The color of joy in a melon and warmth in the desert.
The hue of humility in the sky.

The breath of life in
you and me, the breeze.

Every shade in technicolor,
adorned with cloth, woven in and out
with these very colors to welcome you.

The daughter of this land,
its trees,
the glimmer of its seas in your eyes,
the depth of its forests in your mind,
the strength of its camels in your soles.

The breeze whispered that it was all for me,
this home I can't quite remember.
All this life behind the furtive glance of a barren land.

A memory taken,
a memory passed.

Nour Idris
Wondering: Sudan to Palestine

Sitting behind the TV screen
watching murder be justified live
reminding me of a similar scene
that's been happening with Sudanese lives

I remember
The world watching as we died
not blinking an eye. Meanwhile,
we were fighting for our lives

This has been happening for years
but we took too long to realize it
for Palestine

I can't help but wonder

How time and time again lessons of the past are forgotten
filled with empty declarations

"How could we allow this to happen?"
Knowing,
"We stole land and enslaved stolen people"
"We watched as the nazis killed millions
then proclaimed genocide unrepeatable"

I can't help but wonder
how anyone can justify murdering men, women and children
as if grieving the ones you love isn't a universal burden.

How can we call ourselves allies
when neutrality and saving face is all we prioritize?
How will we only acknowledge the reality of the brutality
years later in a dismissive apology for "this unfortunate tragedy?"

So don't think that you will ever be able to wash
your hands of the blood
you helped shed
the people you helped oppress
the children you helped kill
and the war crimes you hate to condemn.
Ask yourself why

it's only an atrocity when the victims are white
And stop saying "Never forget"
because if you had
thousands of people would still be alive.

But we won't forget
that they ever had to prove their humanity to you
for their treatment to be considered in-humane.

You knew this was all wrong but ignored us when we asked,
"How many more have to die in vain?"

We will fight
for protection against oppression
for freedom
from Gaza to Khartoum.

Sudan bleeds with Palestine
And in time our hearts will heal with Palestine
But that time will never come if silence prevails
and humanity fails.

Hassan Hussein Ibn Ismail
Hope on the Horizon

In the land of Filisteen, where prophets once tread,
Nabi Isa and Nabi Musa, their stories widespread.
Strength in their hearts, like the heroes of old,
Liberators and leaders, courageous and bold.

From Filisteen's soil, a great nation did rise,
Nur Zhengi and Salahudeen, with determined eyes.
Faced with the tide of oppression's might,
In their stare, a fierce resolve, ready to fight.
They fought with valor, never to run away
A legacy of courage that still lights our way.

Oh Gazans, martyrs, resilient and true,
Your strength echoes loudly, a testament through.
In the face of hardship, you stand tall and strong,
For your faith and your people, you've endured for so long.

Imam Mahdi, your avenging liege,
For you, my dear Gazans, hope is on the horizon.
At hand, is your peace, a sweet, gentle breeze,
Uniting our hearts, bringing comfort and ease.
The Prophet, Sallahu Alayhi Wasalaam, proud and near,
Guiding his ummah, wiping away all the tears.
Hold on, dear ones, to the promise divine,
In unity and faith, let your spirits entwine.
For the struggles you face, the world may not see,
But Allah is with you, and His mercy will be your key.

In the footsteps of prophets, you walk with grace,
A living testament, a sacred space.
Ya Gazans, know that you're not alone,
For your resilience and strength, history will be known.

Naqi Rizvi
Ya'aburnee

My children,

replace your blankets   with shrouds,
replace goodnights   with goodbyes
replace your dreams   with the deafening silence
of destruction.

Let your home become your grave
so no one can take away
what was always —
yours.

Anthology Producers and Editors

Sara Bawany is an award-winning poet, author, freelance editor, clinical social worker, and MFA Poetry student at Texas State University. She published *(w)holehearted: a collection of poetry and prose* in 2018, which won Daybreak Press Publishing's "Best Poetry Book" award, and her second book, *Quarter Life Crisis*, was published in October 2023. She is the Managing Editor at Porter House Review and serves as an instructor at House of Amal, a school for young Muslim writers. You can find more of her work on Instagram (@*sara.bawany*) and at www.sarabawany.com.

Amal Kassir is a Syrian-American spoken word poet and activist. She writes and performs poetry that explores themes of identity, culture, social justice, and personal narrative, often drawing on her experiences as a Muslim, Arab-American woman. Kassir has performed at events and festivals worldwide and has been featured in various media outlets. Her poetry is known for its emotional depth, vivid imagery, and powerful commentary on contemporary issues. She published her debut book *Scud Missile Blues* in 2023 and she is the founder of House of Amal, a school for young Muslim writers which you can find at www.houseofamal.co.

Yacoob Manjoo is a South African writer, blogger, and poet. He's published two collections of poetry and prose, and his work has been featured in numerous print and online publications. You can find more of his work on Instagram (@*dreamlife.za*) and his website (dreamlife.wordpress.com).

Anthology Artists

Cover Art

Safia Latif is an oil painter based in California. Her work creatively reimagines Islamic narratives and concepts using visible brushwork and an emphasis on light and color. Latif has pioneered the practice of "Islamicate Impressionism," a novel style that is recognizably painterly and conceptually draws on the social and cultural phenomena associated with the Muslim world from Morocco to Indonesia. Latif earned an MA in Middle Eastern Studies and began a PhD in religion, focusing on the notion of piety as a form of social capital for Muslim women in the medieval world. You can find more of her work at www.safialatif.com or on Instagram (*@safialatifpaintings*)

Cover Design

Michaya Toni is a multifaceted force weaving creativity, spirituality, and healing into her life's work. She is a wife, mother and intuitive expressionist, whose story unfolds as an inspirational Youtuber, poet and abstract artist. Since childhood, writing has been her sanctuary—a steadfast companion and compass in navigating life's challenges. Her journey into poetry and public speaking began at the tender age of 9 years old, when she delivered her first speech. This early exploration laid the foundation for a lifelong passion for the arts that has since led her to many extraordinary places. In her writing, Michaya delves into the beauty of nature, the sovereignty of God, self-love and the intricate workings of the human mind. Having faced her own hardships, Michaya now walks a purposeful path towards healing and helping others. With her unique blend of creativity, spirituality, and empathy, she aims to uplift everyone she encounters on their journey toward wellness and self-discovery. Michaya invites you to join her exploration of faith on YouTube @MichayaToni, where she provides a platform for discussion, understanding and connection. She is also sharing her poetry on Instagram and TikTok @MichayaToni.

Contributors

Amiira Afia is a Muslim South Asian writer based in Dallas, Texas. She is a mental health counselor who uses writing as an avenue to advocate for mental health awareness, specifically within minority communities. Amiira Afia also explores topics related to the preservation of generational identity, and the intersectionality of nature and the human condition. She is currently composing a collection of poems that reflect her life experiences. You can find more of Amiira Afia's work on Instagram (*@amiira.writes*).

Saniya Ruqiah Ahmed began her journey as a spoken word and slam poet in the realm of social justice advocacy. For nearly a decade, her art has been kept within the ears of her audience, and she now aims to bring her work to paper. Her poetry centers on themes like family, faith, social justice, and the Muslim and Indian diaspora. Now as a medical student in the Midwest, her poetry also encompasses humanity and dignity in healthcare. She was a member of 2023 House of Amal cohort. You can find her forthcoming work, *Hum Dum,* with Strange Inc. Publishing.

Sundus Aladra is a California-born, everywhere-raised writer of Palestinian origin. Writing has been one of her most steadfast companions in the face of life's unpredictable ups and downs, and she thinks we all could use a little more of it in our worlds. Sundus's academic background is in the field of Political Science and International Relations. In her free time, she can be found trying to juggle and blend her professional pursuits with her wide expanse of creative hobbies. You can find her on Instagram (*@sunst.arts*).

Salma Alduais holds a background in clinical research and received her undergraduate degree in Human Biology from Michigan State University. Her coursework in literature and bioethics sparked an interest in examining the implications of healthcare inequities, especially in access to treatment abroad. She hopes to pursue a career in medicine. When she's not engaged in her scientific pursuits, she enjoys reading and spending time with family and friends.

Tajuddin "Taj" Ashaheed is a community activist, writer/speaker, and devout Muslim. He has a professional background in market research and criminal justice. Taj is also a blogger, branding consultant, and a former editorial writer for *The Denver Post*, as well as a podcast host. While Taj can be found all over social media, his poetry can be found at: tajverse.blogspot.com. In his spare time, Taj can be found training and competing in MMA, writing and performing spoken word, and chasing after his toddler son.

Naazia Husain Azhar is a writer, physician and mom of four.

Zaheera Badat hails from Pietermaritzburg, South Africa. She is a mother of two incredible daughters and two furry ragdolls, as well as a wife to her best friend. With a penchant for the literary arts, Zaheera is a poet, writer, and qualified copy editor. She is also an academic researcher with a Master's degree in Educational Leadership and Management. Vocationally, she is a registered counselor, personal mastery consultant, and youth mentor. She is a creative confectioner, food stylist, and innovator in the culinary arts. Above all, she is an activist and ardent supporter of marginalized communities.

Shaziya Barkat is a writer based in Dallas, Texas. Her work explores themes including faith, spiritual renewal, love, loss, and mental health. *knowing You*, her first collection of poetry, prose, personal narratives and essays, was published in July 2019 and became a #1 Bestseller as well as the Poetry Book of the Year by Daybreak Press. In 2021, Shaziya published *Doctor Diaries*, followed by the *My Iman Journal: 52-Week Reflection, Gratitude, & Dua Journal* in 2022. In 2024, Shaziya published her debut bestselling children's book *Rahma Dreams of Jannah*. Aside from writing, Shaziya works as a pharmacist. Stay updated with Shaziya's work on Instagram (*@s.s.barkat*).

Basheerah Bulbulia is a 24-year-old aspiring poet who resides in the small town of Koster in South Africa. She is a student of Islamic knowledge and is in the process of memorizing the Quran. Her work is most often inspired by her faith. You can read more of her poems on her Instagram (*@bash26_*) and X (*@basheerah26*). Her poem in this collection is her first published poetry piece.

Warren Clementson was born and raised in London and resides in the UK. He graduated from the University of the Arts London in Film. After working across various television companies, he completed his PGCE and QTS to become a primary school teacher. Due to his lived experience as a Black British, Muslim, neurodivergent man, Warren's poems cover a tapestry of themes. His writing has been showcased at events in *Rumi's Cave* and *Barbican*, alongside features in publications such as *Flint*, *Thawra*, and *From Whispers to Roars*. He is working on his first collection, which explores faith, violence and mental health.

Sara Farhat is a Lebanese poet and educator residing in Canada. She draws inspiration from immersing herself in nature and has a deep appreciation for Arabic poetry, flowers, and trees. Sara enjoys using metaphors and uses her ability to create vivid imagery in her readers' minds. Her self-published chapbook, *Bouquet of Feelings*, showcases the building of a bouquet through a spectrum of emotions. Beyond writing, she enjoys reading, hiking, crocheting, soccer, and photography. You can find her work on Instagram (*@smilesofsunshine*).

Anam Fatima is a mother, homemaker, amateur calligraphy artist, and a published poet from India. She finds beauty in simplicity and loves tea. Her first two collections of poems were published when she was still at school, while her third book, *Nascent Poetry*, was published in 2018. She has worked as a content writer and an administrator for an Islamic school. Her latest obsession is reading Urdu novels and practicing Arabic calligraphy. She's also active on Instagram (*@anamscape*).

Mariam M. Gadala, author of *The Stories in Her Eyes*, enjoys writing creatively, after more than a decade of teaching. She has taught academic writing, history, educational leadership, and language arts to university and high-school students in various cities across three continents. Mariam is a proud wife and mother of three. She holds a Bachelor of International Relations & English Language from the University of British Columbia, along with a Master of Education in Educational Administration & Leadership. Mariam's second poetry book, Jannat, has just been released; follow her on Instagram (@mariam.m.gadala) for updates and more poetry.

Noorul Islam Hammad, an accomplished entrepreneur, is the CEO and co-founder of a pioneering food tech startup in South India, leveraging AI and ML to transform the food industry. An alumnus of the prestigious Indian Institute of Management, he holds a master's in business administration. Beyond business, Hammad is a passionate writer who believes in the transformative power of words. His poetry often explores themes of philosophy and self-awareness. Hammad shares his writings in both English and Urdu on Instagram (*@hammad.nih5*), inspiring hearts and minds alike.

Hassan Hussein Ibn Ismail, a Union Electrician and dedicated farmer, intertwines his passion for poetry with a commitment to social justice. With over three decades of experience, he began his journey in spoken word contests during the early 2000s. Currently, Hassan is immersed in writing three poetry books, including *No Place Safe*, which addresses the ongoing genocide in Palestine. Though he has yet to publish, his words resonate with a deep sense of purpose and a desire to illuminate the struggles of the oppressed.

Nour Idris is a young Sudanese-American visual artist. When she was struggling to express how she felt after witnessing tragedies in Sudan and Palestine, she took to the brush. When that wasn't enough, she took to the pen. Seeing the similarities between the suffering of her people in Sudan and those in Palestine inspired her to write in solidarity, because the path to freedom is paved in unity. Find her work on Instagram and TikTok (*@floornourart* and *@letsdoit_nour*).

Nahida Izzat is a Palestinian living in exile since 1967. She was born in Al-Quds (Jerusalem) and was forced to leave her homeland as a refugee at the age of seven, during the Six-Day War. She holds a B.Sc. in Mathematics, and is a former math teacher, a mother and a grandmother, and a poet. Visit her website at nahidaexiledpalestinian.com.

Lana Kamel is a Syrian high school student living in the US. She believes that writing has the power to heal wounds, and wishes to share its medicine with the world.

Walid Kessal is a firm believer in a one-state solution called Palestine, where justice prevails from the river to the sea. He enjoys communicating with machines and human beings. He works as a software developer and holds a master's degree in Microelectronics. He is also pursuing a bachelor's degree in Technical English. In poetry, he found a friend who would always accompany and support him in journeys to find the light in the heart of darkness. He's currently working on his first poetry manuscript, and is also working on a project called *VoiceTheWords*.

Tehreem Khalid is a Canadian poet. She was born in Pakistan and grew up in Saudi Arabia. She currently works as a radiation therapist, treating patients with cancer. Being a woman in STEM, she understands the power of words, and is passionate about writing and storytelling. When she isn't immersed in a book or a K-drama, she can be found hanging out with her cats, learning to swim, and practicing kick-boxing. She also enjoys exploring the Canadian Rockies, especially during summer. Tehreem occasionally posts her writing on Instagram (@*tehreem.thepoet*).

Oliver Khan is a Muslim writer of Pakistani origin who was raised in the American Midwest. He received his MFA in creative writing from the University of Pittsburgh in 2005. His poems have appeared in *The Dewdrop*, *Chicago Reader*, *Gargoyle*, and elsewhere. He practices law and lives in Lombard, Illinois with his family.

Layanne is a Palestinian-American Muslim writer, poet, and biochemist. Layanne was first introduced to the world of poetry at the age of 17 and has been captivated ever since. Her work centers around Palestinian culture, Islamic spirituality, and a deep connection to community and the environment.

Hadee Krad is a Syrian American guitarist who grew up in Chicago. He currently lives in Las Vegas.

Ray Lacina is an English professor and writer based in Michigan. He completed his Ph.D. in American Literature at the University of Toronto, and began his formal teaching career in Saudi Arabia (after brief excursions into corporate Canada), before landing his current gig teaching college writing and literature in 2002. He's published a novel and a collection of poetry, and also been featured in other publications. You can find more of his work on Instagram (*@raylacina*).

Jaweerya Mohammad is a passionate educator, having taught Middle School English for many years. Her writing is shaped by her Muslim and first-generation Pakistani American identity. She's been published in Renard Press's *Third Space* anthology, and has more poems coming in literary magazines such as *Overtly Lit* and *Poetry Breakfast*. She firmly believes in the power of words, and that story-telling can foster a more empathetic and just world. You can find more of her work on Instagram (*@jaweeryajournals*).

Salma Mohammad is a Palestinian-Egyptian American poet and writer. She is best known for winning the 2019 National Student Poet Award in 2019 for her piece "White Noise", which centers on the desensitization of violence in Southwest Asian and North African countries. Her work revolves around themes of liberation, diaspora, and identity.

Noha Nasri is a writer and poet, born in Canada and currently residing in the United States. She is the author of *Iridescence*, a collection of poetry and prose that delves into the soul to capture the realities of life. It is an emotional journey that embraces love and loss; and at its core, it shines a light on the power of perception. *Iridescence* is available from Barnes & Noble, Amazon, and Books-A-Million. She is also active on Instagram (*@noha_nasri*).

Sana Nimer is a writer of poetry, lyric, and spoken word, currently based in Washington, D.C. Her work is influenced by her faith-centric upbringing and her outlook as a Muslim American woman on the cusp of Generations Y and Z. It is also deeply inspired by a sum of her most cherished moments: time spent in her native country of Palestine. Sana's writing explores themes of justice and resilience, diaspora and occupation, privilege and purpose, and introspection and connection (both social and divine). You can find more of her work and follow her journey into authorship on Instagram (*@spokenbysana*).

Kate Rafiq is an award-winning children's author, illustrator, and indie-publisher currently living in Mid Wales, U.K, with her husband and four children. So far, she has created three picture books: *Birmingham Boy*, *The World is Your Masjid* (Winner of the Muslim Bookstagram Award for Best Early Picture Book 2021, and translated into Bahasa in 2024), and *We Are Here* (shortlisted for *The Little Rebels Award* 2024). Find out more at dunebooks.co.uk.

Naqi Rizvi, a Toronto-based poet, began his poetic journey influenced by his father's passion for Urdu poetry. While his roots lie in Urdu's rich poetic tradition, his North American upbringing channeled his poetic expression into English. Naqi's poetry delves into topics such as faith, spirituality, cultural experience, and identity, often paying homage to Prophet Muhammed (peace be upon him) and his Household (Allah be pleased with them). Being a software engineer by profession, Naqi writes poems for both humans and machines. Find more of his work on Instagram (*@naqisqalam*).

Wajiha Rizvi is based in Austin and is the daughter of Pakistani immigrants. Her writing sits at the intersection of identity, social justice, home, and horror. She was a participant in *Rosa Rebellion's* inaugural *COMPOSE* cohort – a storytelling incubator for women of color. She recently completed her first manuscript, titled *Ghosts of All of Them*, telling the story of a family's displacement during the Partition of India in 1947, narrated by a churail: a demoness in South Asian folklore. Her writing has been featured in *Brown History*. You can find more of her work on Substack (*@wajihasultana*).

Nehan Shujaat is a Pakistani-American poet, artist, and registered nurse. She focuses on indulging in her passion for art and poetry, having written and illustrated her poetry book, *Here's the Chai*. Her writing themes often revolve around the medical field, her experience as a first-generation Pakistani, and her Islamic spirituality. Apart from writing and performing poetry, she is an oil painter, leaning heavily toward an impressionistic style.

Hajara Zaheed is a poet and student from Sri Lanka. Currently pursuing a B.Sc in Environment, Development and Sustainability at the University of Colombo, she spends her downtime reading books, creating art, and penning down poems across a variety of themes. She is an aspiring author, driven by a strong love for nature, social justice, art and poetry. "Gazans of Paradise" marks her debut poem published in print. Follow her writing journey on Instagram (@one_page_later).

Safiyah Zaidi is a freelance writer and aspiring law student interested in human and civil rights, and constitutional law. Through prose and poetry, she loves to explore themes related to gender equity and international justice. Her other work explores culture, politics, and media. Her article about the deliberate targeting of Gazan journalists and media literacy has been published in *The Conversationalist*. She is currently based in Washington, DC.

Acknowledgments

With boundless gratitude, we honor all who made this anthology a reality. Since our inception, we have aspired to create a collection echoing the powerful voices of our community—students, collaborators, and teachers. By the grace of Allah, this dream became possible, furthering a purpose far greater than ourselves.

Our heartfelt appreciation first goes to Yacoob Manjoo, South African writer and cherished member of the House of Amal community, who rekindled our vision for publishing an anthology in December 2023. Inspired by the overwhelming entries from our "Poems for Palestine" winter contest, Yacoob offered his expertise to shape these profound works into a published anthology. This collection stands as a testament to his foresight and dedication.

We are deeply honored that renowned Palestinian-American poet Naomi Shihab Nye graciously penned the Foreword. Her extraordinary talent and unending generosity enrich all who learn from her.

Our sincere thanks extend to our House of Amal Cohort 2 students— Sundus Aladra, Zainab Hashmi, Bayan Fares, Layanne Khaskia, Michaya Toni, and Walid Kessal—whose diligent participation in multiple rounds of editing brought these poems to life. Each of them graduates from our Cohort with nearly complete poetry manuscripts of their own.

Special appreciation is due to our dedicated team members: Salma Mohammad, Walid Kessal, and Michaya Toni, for their tireless work behind the scenes.

We are honored to present on our cover a painting titled *The Ummah* by Islamicate Impressionist artist, Safia Latif. This visionary piece, amongst her many others, beautifully captures the spirit of unity and resilience.

With heartfelt appreciation, we extend our gratitude to our beloved community and to the many gifted contributors whose stunning poetry has brought new depth and grace to this charitable initiative.

Finally, special thanks go to the Zakat Foundation for their crucial work in Palestine and across the globe, fostering hope and support where it's most needed. May Allah accept this humble offering and bless our collective efforts.

About House of Amal

House of Amal was founded in July 2020 in the throes of the COVID-19 global pandemic. Seeking a foster home for the creative spirit and a writing community, founder Amal Kassir began to teach the weekly writing hour on Wednesdays at 11 am cst via Instagram Live, which quickly attracted hundreds of interested participants.

Since then, House of Amal has evolved into a well-rounded writing school for the Muslim creative. We teach a 12-month curriculum of writing to our cohort students, have now published our first community anthology, run several membership groups that include intensive editing and critique workshopping, continue with virtual open mics, community workshops, and so much more.

None of this would be possible without YOU, our community of students, readers, and leaders. We are grateful for your support knowing that together, we can build a home for the Muslim creative.

100% of the proceeds of this book will go to Zakat Foundation of America's urgent appeal for Gaza. We urge you to buy this book directly from its source and/or from independent local booksellers.

May Allah accept from you and from us.

About Zakat Foundation of America

Zakat Foundation of America, in essence, is the spiritual energy created by the meeting of two prayers:

1. It the earnest plea of a sincere giver who asks God to let the resources He has given one do good in the world.
2. The urgent entreaty of someone in need asking God for help.

That spiritual energy is called servanthood. Servanthood is the founding ethic of the Zakat Foundation. Servanthood is the condition that the people who direct, staff, and support the Zakat Foundation strive for. We seek to serve our One Creator by serving all of His creation.

This is the state we at Zakat Foundation aspire to live in. We strive to be builders for the benevolent — those who dream of a better world for the near and the far neighbor to live together in as one.

Serving our givers. Serving our receivers. Serving our Zakat Foundation workers and volunteers — all in the service of our One Lord, and ever at His pleasure. This is the ethos of the Zakat Foundation of America.

Zakat Foundation of America's directors and staff believe the eradication of poverty and inequality on earth is not only possible; it is a mandate of Islam upon us and, therefore, a necessarily achievable goal in our lifetimes.

For this reason, we enthusiastically seek new knowledge, partnerships, ways, and ideas to develop our humanitarian vision, improve our charitable outreach, refine our philanthropic strategies and approach, and, most importantly, grow and expand our inclusive Zakat Foundation family.

Since 2001, we have provided life-saving assistance to families in Gaza and the West Bank. In collaboration with local partners, Zakat Foundation has delivered critical relief, including food, water, and healthcare, during times of crisis. In 2023, our efforts—such as the 1 Million Meals campaign, rice airdrops, truck shipments, soup kitchens, food and water distribution, and winter relief packages—benefited over 1.2 million people in Gaza. These initiatives are designed to meet immediate needs and create a foundation for long-term regional stability and resilience.

Zakat Foundation's ongoing programs focus on sustainable recovery. Through Livelihood program support, we help families rebuild through agriculture and income-generating projects. The Healthcare and Well-Being program provides life-saving treatments for pediatric cancer patients, and the Orphan Care program offers food, education, healthcare, and emotional support to children affected by the conflict. Seasonal Giving ensures families have nourishing food and supplies during Ramadan, Udhiyah/Qurbani and winter seasons. These initiatives ensure that even in the most challenging times, the most vulnerable populations have the resources they need to survive and thrive.

Looking ahead, the Zakat Foundation of America is committed to continuing its vital work in Gaza and the West Bank, working closely with local partners to support ongoing recovery and reconstruction. Our programs remain a lifeline for Palestinian families, helping them rebuild their futures and ensuring children have access to the opportunities they deserve. Support for our work can make a lasting impact, bringing hope and relief to those who need it most.

www.ingramcontent.com/pod-product-compliance
Lightning Source LLC
Chambersburg PA
CBHW030459130626
46549CB00007B/2786